HEARTSTRINGS <3
&
HASHTAGS

70 poems about love, dating, heartbreak and self-love

Marisa Hawkes

First published in Great Britain in 2024
[ISBN 978-1-7384589-7-4]

Printed on demand in order to reduce waste and environmental impact.

For inquiries, or collaboration, please contact:
heartstringshashtags@gmail.com

To all my wonderful friends around the world, whose experiences, wise advice, and hilarious one-liners brought so many of these poems to life. You know who you are.

To mum and dad, thank you for giving me endless moments to write about and for being a constant source of love and support.

To my twin flame <3 You make it so easy to write about love.

And to everyone facing tough times: may these poems lift you, comfort you, and bring a smile to your face when you need it most. You are not alone. You deserve respect. You deserve love.

Contents

love

♥♥♥♥♥♥♥♥♥♥♥

kind love exists

he calms my
overactive gemini brain
by listening
while i talk
my love language is physical touch
his is quality time
i found a man
who says what he means
and means what he says
isn't that rare these days?
four years strong
i must have done a lot wrong
in my past life
to get it so right this time
but before you get jealous
he sometimes snores at night
that's a beige flag alright

#NoRedFlags

temporary insanity

he is the ultimate aphrodisiac
each moment with him
etched into my breath
his face invades my thoughts
my legs twitch
under the table
anticipating
his voice
down the corridor
i did not know
you could miss someone
after just ten minutes
i bite my nails
waiting
desire and lust
hold me hostage
i am his prisoner
chained to his side
until his green eyes
tell me otherwise

#Surrender

mr.big

aren't we all like carrie bradshaw?
searching for our mr.big
our hype man
our king
to feel that za-za-zu
and never settle
to risk getting hurt
to be illogical
but in the quest for true love
carrie might have been right
our girlfriends are our soulmates
while guys bring us a little delight
the lesson we must learn
is to love who we are
before we can share
our hearts with another

#LoveYourselfFirst

mr.darcy

my life feels like austen on rewind
first impression of you? "what a knob"
but like mr.darcy, you were misunderstood
behind that front, a heart of gold stood
yearning for love, your true self shone
in time, your sincerity warmed my own
you were from a dream, and i was shook
now we're a couple, just like in the book
pride and prejudice taught us to reflect
about mutual respect
a love we must protect
don't judge a book by its cover
there's more to see when you take time to discover

#TimelessRomance

wuthering heights

as kids
we used to climb trees
inseparable
the woods didn't care
who we were
we looked for one another
like cathy and heathcliff
because i was poorer than you
others frowned on our love
but we knew
"whatever our souls are made of
his and mine are the same"
we might be from different worlds
but we spoke the same
you moved on
i did too
but years later
i still missed the fire
that burning desire

#AllConsumingLove

heartstopper

charlie and nick
their love story is so sweet
i "aww" at the TV screen
what they share is innocent, pure
i learnt a lot from them for sure

struggling to know how to feel
but growing into who they're meant to be
a reminder that love, when true
is brave, and finds its way through

#CharlieAndNick

love songs

my dad always said
that 99% of songs
are about love
and i think he's right
every song i hear
is about it
in one way or another
day and night
mostly about heartbreak

when my love ended
i couldn't turn on the radio
i had love-song anxiety
fearing what i'd hear
the chances of a love song
felt like 100 to 1
too near

so i deleted spotify
and quickly fled the store
if *wildest dreams* came on
i couldn't take it anymore
even youtube wasn't safe
i had to keep my itchy fingers
away from the internet's lure

but then a friend said
music can heal you
help you process your feelings
and endure
so i listened and listened
and felt my emotions rise
music expressed
what i couldn't understand
and brought me back to life

music helped me come back
to myself
when i thought i would disappear
never to be found again
but now i listen without a single tear

#MusicIsHealing

long distance love

i have so much to offer
to anyone in my life
and especially to you
despite the distance
you got the job you wanted
(one you enjoy)
and i wanted to move
to be by your side
that was always the plan
to be together, no matter what
face-to-face
in the same place
so we wouldn't have to do
the long-distance thing
you said you looked forward
to being with me again
so we can experience
life and all it brings

#WeCanMakeItWork

twin flames

it took breaking
to find you
to embark
on another journey
of transformation
to learn
to love myself
to no longer give love freely
to those who did not deserve it
a love so sincere
a bond destined
you taught me lessons
no one else could
you said
face adversity
i said
love deeply
we did not need words
to understand
you saw me
i saw you
a mirror reflected back
a connection
that transcends time and space
in this lifetime
or the next
men in black could erase our memories
but we would find each other
again and again
my eternal twin

#SoulConnection

living for this

being loved by you
is like tasting my favourite ice cream
being loved by you
is being mesmerised by my cat's blue eyes
being loved by you
is hearing the waves lapping against the shore
being loved by you
is feeling the warming brilliance of the sun
being loved by you
is like wearing technicolour glasses
being loved by you
is like smelling home cooking
being loved by you
makes life feel worth living

#DefinitelyRecommend

just the way you are

so you have acne?
he doesn't care
you're clumsy?
he likes it
you think you look fat?
he thinks you look fit
you like to do silly dances?
it makes him smile
you're lazy?
he thinks it's cute

he doesn't care because...
he likes you for you

#YouArePerfect

golden retriever energy

a golden retriever, that's what you are
you're the best friend a girl could ask for!
when i look into your eyes, i melt
a warm feeling i've never felt
sadness or anger don't hang around me long
with you beaming at me, things can't go wrong!
when you goof around, i can't help but grin
your playful charm pulls me in
you're loyal and cheerful, through and through
every tail's wagging
i'm so lucky to have you

#GoldenRetrieverBoyfriend

my happy place

he asked where my happy place was
i said: "you know - the beach"
i asked him the same question
he said: "wherever you are"
aww, ain't love sweet!

#RightAnswer

puppy love

being in love with you
feels like we're back at high school
doodling a love heart
on the corner of my notebook
holding hands
under the table
playing footsie
sneaking away at lunch
for a kiss
behind the shed
feeling flustered beside you
i notice the other girls
looking at you
wondering how a girl like me
landed a cute guy like you

#YoungLove

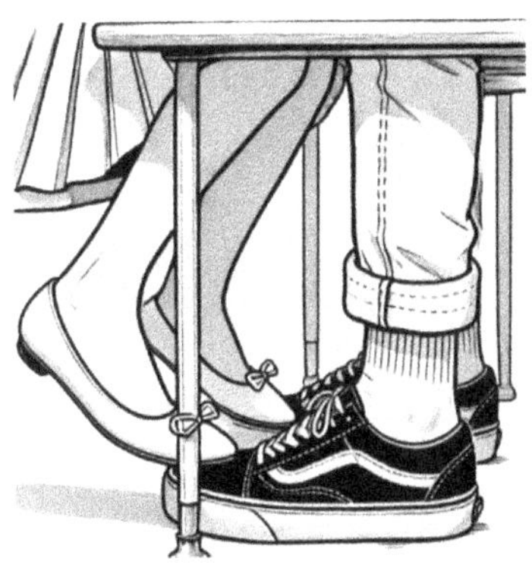

comfortable silence

we sit together reading books
together-but-silent
side-by-side
on our purple sofa

all you can hear is that swish sound
as each page rubs against our thumbs

i had never known peace like this
the silence is absolute bliss

#NoWordsNeeded

pet names

i love when he calls me piggy
every time he says it
i get all giggly
i call him 'bitte'
'cause of an M&S card
we laughed so hard
we were caught off guard
now it's framed, a work of art
each name a little secret we keep
a childish code, nothing too deep
tiny echoes that make my heart sing
because joy lives in silly things!

#SillyBilly

spotify playlists

we share this amazing talent of
visualising scenes from a movie of our life
to certain songs, that feel created just for us
adding to our spotify playlist is
a love language only we are fluent in
hours on the sofa, lost in sound
wrapped up in each other
listening to dreamy, melodic edm
soft kisses in the spaces between beats
just vibing to music that feels otherworldly

we have a playlist for every year
since we fell in love
a timeline in songs
like jack and jack's *no one compares to you*
laughing at the chipmunk voice
too many inside jokes
tucked into those notes

and we dream of that road trip to america
still high on the bucket list
windows down, volume up
our playlist carrying us through miles of fun
a promise...a vision of us driving in the sun

#SpotifyPlaylists

me (unfiltered version)

i don't need to wear a filter
for you to see me
in my onesie
glasses on
makeup-free
grumpy taking out the bins
or stumbling over my own feet
there is no need to hide the days
when tears blur my eyes
when my body clicks and aches
even when i am undone
you love me
i'm safe

loving someone is easy
when life is good
but loving someone
when life is tough
that is something rare and true
and worth everything
to hold onto

#FlawsAndAll

dating

♡♡♡♡♡♡♡♡♡♡♡

lover girl era

since he slid into my dms
being his girl is my favourite occupation
loving him is my full-time aspiration
in him, i've found my forever destination
he's my favourite, my number one
taking polaroids, dreaming of kids to come
i'll be his groupie, certified for life
obsessed with him - yes, i'll be his wife
my love gps never goes astray
perhaps i'll teach you how someday

#Obsessed

emotionally mature man

he communicates his feelings
gently
i never have to guess
or read between the lines
he never tells me
what to wear
he loves how i shine
i never worry
i might say the wrong thing
no treading on eggshells
no second-guessing
he doesn't mind
if i have male friends
no jealousy
our trust transcends
he always walks beside me
never leaves me behind
a man who knows
that love is gentle and kind

#PrinceCharming

love on the gram

i'm whipped af
my ride or die
it hits differently
he's my sweet high
i soft launched my bf
while sabrina went full steam
his voice puts me in my feels
living in my head rent-free
great day to go viral
for being in love
i manifested this
being his lover girl
has me caught in a swirl

#InstaLove

opposites can attract

he is chill
i am fire
he's savoury
i'm sweet
i cook
he eats
he's kombucha
i'm pumpkin spice latte
i like to go out
he likes to stay in
a blend of opposites
that somehow meet
but he won't be caught dead
...doing karaoke!

#YinAndYang

digital love

mondays are
a new match on tinder
deciding
if the vibe feels right
tuesdays are
for the meme exchange
sending tiktoks and gifs
to keep the convo alive
wednesdays
are for getting excited
over midweek texts
thursdays are
thinking of things we can do
deciding on a nice place with a view
fridays are
for the late-night drive
playlist blasting
in a parked car
saturdays are
for brunch dates
iced lattes and boujee cakes
sundays are
for oversized hoodies
watching netflix
lost in our favourite movies

#TinderellaStory

lost in translation

a japanese man once told me
"your beauty is illegal"
i said "arigato"
and laughed
nobody in england
would say that
funny how flattery
can be beautiful in broken english
like when a waiter
brought me dessert
and said "you are so sweet"
i thought he meant me!
but it was the cake
for me to eat
i dated a guy from ukraine
he said, "you have a body for sin"
i laughed and thanked him right then
didn't make sense
but ladies, any compliment's a win!

#JustTakeIt

go slow

take your time
don’t rush
or give everything away
offer a little
and see if you get
something back
don’t close yourself off
to what this relationship could be
but take your time
and let it develop naturally

#GentleReminder

this charming man

he likes batman and marvel
believes anyone can be a hero

he has a charm that's magnetic
his touch is telekinetic
he walks in a room
and his energy goes boom

his aura is lovely
plus, he's really cuddly
he can braid girls' hair
this guy - he's so rare!

#BatBae

summer fling

how did i go from being okay on my own
to craving him in every shape and form
wanting him in ways i've never wanted anyone before
filling my time with anything that consumes my brain
trying everything i can to numb the pain
a summer fling that's hard to forget
but i don't want to, it's too good to put to rest
i know i'll see him again
but the waiting keeps me wide awake
unable to sleep, lust pumping through my veins
wondering why he's different from the rest
is it his lips, his eyes, the feeling he leaves in my chest?
whatever it is, i'm completely obsessed
it was a summer fling i never want to forget

#HolidayRomance

Contributed by Tara Formosa

situationships aren't it

i met a 25 yo in a bar,
we got to talking...
she spoke of dating in 2024
the endless grind
no commitment
just wasted time
"we swipe, we text"
she says
"but it's all a game
no one wants to settle
it's always the same"
i said
"my girlfriends and i
we too
are tired and bored
of half-hearted love
and being ignored
being ghosted is rude!
we crave connection
something that sticks
not just a fling
or being sent dick pics!"

#Situationships

date night

it's saturday night
you pick me up
in your old tin ride
sorry hyundai
matching outfits
we look cute
holding hands
you tell a joke
making fun of
something woke
what do you fancy?
street food's the best!
time flies when i'm
with this smiley man
my phone’s on silent
no interruptions tonight
hours fly by
wish we could pause time

#LoverBoy

more than mid

he's a 10,
but i'd rather a 5
i'll tell you girls why
a 10 thinks he's god's gift to the earth
all looks, no depth
if he's a 9, probably too much charm
an 8? forget it, probably still shallow
checking out their own shadow
a 7's still caught up in his own hype
talks big game, but it doesn't feel right
if he's a 6, maybe there's hope
a 5 though?
now that's the sweet spot
cares about your mind
not what cup size you've got
some things are more important than looks
give me someone who's read a few books
who laughs at my jokes, gets who i am
not another token beefcake from the gym
because love's not about chasing a score
it's about finding someone who sees so much more

#LooksArentEverything

perfect doesn't exist

the perfect person doesn't exist
but still we chase the disney dream
we want:
good looks
someone smart
and witty too
don't forget the romance
chemistry
someone who's true
we want a best friend
someone who makes us feel safe
someone who respects us
treats us kind
a little bit rich
to spoil us like a princess

c'mon girls let's be realistic

#NobodyIsPerfect

commitment phobe

she has a seduction to her
men fall for her with ease
she lures them in with sincerity
then drops them like the breeze
she's not the type to date
she's a player through and through
she only craves the casual
a fleeting touch...
a glance
she moves in and out of lives
never giving love a chance

#ScaredOfLove

left on unread

love nowadays is a battlefield
waiting a week for your reply
not knowing what to say
the two black ticks taunt me
instead of just telling me no
you run away
ghosting is the coward's way out
what's wrong with this generation?
why are we so quick to flee?
why do we play games
choosing to purposely delay
hiding behind phone screens
being left on unread
or, was it something I said?

#ByeBoyBye

pornhub

i swear porn is rotting the brains
of all the young men today

addicted and an xxx-holic
a doom scroller
with a endless boner

they want a pornstar
not a lady
women want to be adored
not disrespected or degraded

pornhub can't teach them
the things that really count
like respect and consent

we need to break this cycle fast
so better sex ed can actually last

#SexEducationMatters

heartbreak

♡♡♡♡♡♡♡♡♡♡♡

love and loss

i heard a quote i loved
“that which you have cherished
with all your heart
you can never lose”
they say it is better
to have loved and lost
than never to have loved at all
this is true
at least for me
and maybe for you?
without the pain
you can’t know the joy
without the rain
the flowers won’t grow
without the lows
you won’t feel the highs
it’s in the dark
that we see ourselves rise

#LoveAndGrowth

<3

my heart's a funny thing
a powerful muscle
i can't reason with
it wants what it wants
my brain knows better
when it opens up to someone new
it risks everything
heartache
heartbreak
but despite this
this organ will always heal

#HeartFelt

one day

why can't we
be more than friends?
like emma and dexter
the timing
is never right
i am so grounded
you are so carefree
that frustrates the f out of me

sometimes you piss me off
but you are always there
year after year
why do we try so hard
to find love
when we don’t need to…
what you are looking for
is right under your nose

#TimingIsEverything

love triangle

one was my head
the other my heart
why when i had a good thing going
did i have to checkmate myself?
if i told my mum i was in love with two men
she'd tell me i'd gone insane
how do you choose
when both feel right?
torn between what is
and what could be
i'm low key obsessed
with both of their charms
feels like i'm swiping left
on each of their hearts
what do i do?
should i play the two?
but someone always gets hurt

#HotMess

watch out for the waves

falling in love is like surfing
sometimes everything flows perfectly
and other times you crash
hard

#LoveIsLikeThis

catch and release

like a tiger
he loved the thrill
of the chase
when he caught his prey
(little old me)
he lost interest

dating can feel like
a cat and mouse game
the texting stops
the waiting begins

#ThrillOfTheChase

excuses

"i just want you to be happy" he says
"even if it's not with me..."
like a martyr
like it's for my sake
- but it's just an excuse
to end 3 years with me
"to give you up is a sacrifice" he says
another excuse disguised as kindness
- but it's just a way to
leave, and be free of guilt

#NoMoreExcuses

love's stream

just because we break up
doesn't mean the love stops
just because i don't like you
doesn't mean i stop loving you
until the tap is turned off
the water will keep flowing

love is like this
a stream of powerful emotions
that take time to cool off
it might dry out
but it will turn on again

#LoveIsLike

goodbye my lover

we found each other
sweet surrender
eyes full of wonder

you were everything i ever asked for
but then you came
you went
you saw

now you're gone
tell me where it went wrong
i'm trying to figure out where
your love
disappeared from...

here one minute
goodbye
whats next?

the day is torture
my heart aches
i feel ill without you
i shiver, i shake

i wish i could hold you
but now it's too late

#Heartache

energy vampires

i feel like i have an antenna
attracting bad energy to me
they want what I have
(something they lack)
my light draws them in
like a moth to the flame
my soul tries to warn me
that they are no good
but they drain me
and move on...

#BadEnergyStayFarAway

beautiful ruins

all these ruins still standing
after thousands of years
even after earthquakes and volcanoes
the colosseum
the parthenon
the great pyramids
will stand the test of time
they endured
what our love could not
we never had strong foundations
to begin with
so it was only
a matter of time
till we crumbled
and now all we are
are some beautiful ruins
pieces of something
that once was whole
but never meant to last

#PiecesOfUs

cheap talk

you talk the talk
sell dreams
but keep none

just like you pretend to care
about climate change
but you use plastic forks

you say you want a relationship
but you keep scrolling on bumble
you're all about being authentic
but your mouth's writing checks
it can't cash

instead of eyeing up the
latest love island babe
why don't you practice what you preach
stop future-faking
and love-bombing
coz baby, your talk is cheap

#ActionsSpeakLouder

cruise ship love

weeks passed in flirtatious fashion
dancing around our feelings for one another
one night in my cabin
i pretended to be asleep
too nervous to make a move
i felt his breath hovering near my lips
my hair standing on end
waiting for a kiss
but his nerve slipped away
i tried to resist him
wary of falling in love again
scared... what a cliché
but like a drug
i was hooked on him
craving another fix
we took taxis to hidden malls
far from the ship
laughing and goofing
in our own little zone
like teenagers in love
in a world of our own
our hands intertwined
his lips met mine
tender and passionate
like lightning striking my heart
i was breathless
paralysed in a flood
of heightened emotions
electricity coursing through me
in bermuda
a rented scooter and a monsoon
found us at an abandoned bus shelter
drenched
as rain penetrated my skin
into my bones

something sparked an argument
as he clutched my waist
his dark curls matted to his forehead
he shouted through the rain
“i don’t understand”
i stammered
our eyes locked
sitting in silence
on that cold plastic bench
as the rain thudded in my ears
a love unexpected
but undeniable
a fleeting ship romance
one day had to end

#NotMeantToBe

forget closure

i need to he honest with you
sometimes closure does not come
i begged for answers
hoping they would put a stop the pain
but they never did
instead I just drove my friends insane
a lot of people cannot even explain
what they feel
this is why closure isn't the answer
keep pushing through
day by day
you do not need it to move forward

#YouGotThis

stages of a breakup

shock sat with me for weeks
and i'd sit with it...
staring blankly at a white wall
crying until i looked like a bloated frog
my family tensed up, friends grew quiet
i saw it in their faces
but i couldn't do anything about it
i wasn't in denial
i was grieving a death
when you face the reality
of not seeing 'your person' again
the loneliness came in waves
and i'd walk out of work at midday
overwhelmed with panic
the silence of loss suffocating me
then anger flared, sharp and hot
at him, at myself, at time and love lost
i talked through a hundred "what-ifs"
until friends stopped picking up the phone
and then one morning, i woke up in less pain
acceptance slowly washing over me
it might feel like the end of the world right now, but...
be patient
time will heal you and make everything better again

#TrustTheProcess

red flags

red flags in the beginning
are red flags forever
pay attention
to the early warning signs
to avoid crying later
not trying to scare you
but remember
to open your eyes
and listen with intention
they will reveal themselves
quietly...
are you paying attention?
gaslighting
manipulation
possessiveness
and jealousy
remember these
are never okay

#RedFlags

who am i without you?

my mistake was making
my whole life about you
now you're gone
i don't know what to do
with myself
i gave up so much of me...
my hobbies, my dreams, my job
i didn't even realise
until i was on my own

finding a new routine
unlearning waking up at 6 a.m
knowing i won't see your name
pinging on my phone screen
who am i now?
i'm a new me

#FindingMyself

self-love

♥♥♥♥♥♥♥♥♥♥♥

hot girl summer

it's a hot girl summer
with a glow that's all mine
slay all day
living unapologetically
with my main character energy
pink miniskirt
i'm free to flirt
rooftop down
i'm sun-kissed and thriving
living my best life
enjoying good vibes
under the sun's embrace
i love being alive

#VibeCheckPassed

good vibes only

the books say
lift your frequency
focus on what makes you feel good
and live authentically
embrace the positive
chuck out the negative
practice the law of attraction
and manifest what you wish
rhonda wrote
ask and believe
and you shall receive
what are you waiting for?
you are the universe's masterpiece

#RaiseYourVibration

she-ro

my mum always told me:
be your own "she-ro" (hero)
i love that
be in charge of your own happiness
you don't need anyone to save you
save yourself
spare yourself, from all the bs
because, inside you is a hero
who no matter what
will always fight for you

#Shero

short

yes
i am short
5'2 to be exact

all my life
they told me how small i was
as they did my mother
who is even smaller

yes
i can't reach the top shelf
yes
i ask tall strangers for help

but my worth - and yours
was never measured in inches

#StandTall

you are enough

you don't need to find
the other half of yourself
to complete you
you are all you ever need
you are already complete

#YouAreEnough

laugh more

laughter really is the best medicine
kids know this
they smile and giggle
to their heart's content
it's so contagious
i just want to join in!

when you feel down
and don't know what to do
put on a funny film
or talk to someone who's jolly
who can remind you
that we were all kids once

just because we grew up
doesn't mean we should
stop laughing
or stop playing

#LaughterIsGoodForTheSoul

life lesson

the greatest showman
reminded me of a lesson so grand
when searching for your purpose in life
understand
and never forget
that bringing joy to others
is a very special gift!

#LifeLessons101

through the fog

this is not the man you met
his eyes are dead
lost in the fog
of his own mind

if you didn't know about depression
how could you know he was depressed?
you're not a doctor or a psychic
you couldn't have guessed

you have to give him time
until he decides
to come out of it
only he can say
when this storm will pass
just be with him
let him sleep
let him be
you must not think
with your emotions
but with your brain

you have done
all you could
supportive and encouraging
as he seeks help
but now you must
focus on your own path
there's nothing you can do
until his body and mind
decide to leave the fog behind

#PatienceAndLove

therapy helps

i sit in a grey chair
in the therapist's room
sifting through the remains
of my ill-fated relationship
dried mascara all over my face
i think: *what a state...*

judgement followed me everywhere...
"you don't need to pay," they said
"you have us"
but like everything in life
that wouldn't last

kathryn has kind eyes
she doesn't tell me to *get over it*
she lets me feel
lets me be
i realise speaking to someone
outside of your circle
is actually very freeing

here i can sit
feel safe
and unburden myself
i get glimpses of hope
even on bad days

every week
i sit in the grey chair
and see a slow return
of the girl i used to be:
happy, grateful, and free

#TherapyIsCool

moving on

a girl sat on the table next to me
in a local coffee shop
crying her eyes out
was it about a boy? *yes*
...she was having trouble moving on

she was me once
and probably you too
we talked for a while about
the suffering that love brings

we came to the conclusion that:
heartbreak doesn't last
everything is temporary
and we are all worthy of love

#LoveLessons

queen energy

my friend is like a cat in heat
she smells testosterone from down the street

(is that why half the world is a mistake?)

she doesn't fall in love; she's on 'a break'
her favourite mantra is to have fun
"if you've got nothing to add, jog on -
"don't just settle for anyone!"
make sure the juice is worth the squeeze
'cause love can turn sour just like old cheese
and remember
you don't need a king
to know you're a queen

#NoSettling

good advice

my friends say
everything happens for a reason
what a cliché
but they turned out to be right
sometimes someone
is supposed to be in your life
sometimes they're not
people walk in and out
and that's fine

(the ones that are meant to stay, will)

#EverythingHappensForAReason

healing journey

if you're suffering inside
open up and ask for help
be completely honest
embrace the truth
communicate your fears
release your doubt
share your worries
don't live in regret
deal with your feelings
as they arise
don't let them fester
or keep them inside

#HelpIsAvailable

it's okay to not be okay

you are pissed off today
you see people happy on socials
but you know this is fake
there's no way they can be happy all the time
and you know that's fine
some days, you feel fatigued
some days, you don't wanna speak
to anyone or do anything
sometimes you find it hard to be grateful
for the life you currently have
it's okay
you just need some space
to recharge yourself
and then, when tomorrow comes,
you can start again

#TomorrowIsANewDay

you're not a tree

"do you think I should leave him?" I asked my friend
she said "are you a tree?"
puzzled, i laughed and said "no"
she replied," so you can leave, a tree can't do that..."

#RelationshipAdvice

breath of fresh air

sometimes we forget who we are
i'm here to remind you that -
you are a girl boss
a beautiful soul
you are a fearless leader
a breath of fresh air
you are unique
you stand tall like no one
you are empathetic
a queen bee
you are wonder woman
and so much more...

#RememberWhoYouAre

people pleaser

i used to want everyone
to like me
a chronic people pleaser
yup, that was me
so i dealt with drama
and petty games
just to score people's approval
and ignore any shame
but one day it hit me
i learned to say "no"
turning your back on bs
is how you grow

#NoApologies

labels don't define you

society says we're either
too fat or too thin
too sensitive or too cold
too quiet or too bold
too young or too old

family says
you should do this
you should be that
but that's not who you are

you are not your trauma
your illness, or your flaws

stand out instead of fitting in
there's no box they can put you in

#BeYourself

start living today

never lose
your childish enthusiasm
for life
remember life is a blessing
a beautiful trip
don't hold on to the past
or chase the future
that was then
and this is now
you are a different person
this time around
play more
dance more
paint or sing
or run really fast for no reason
because it's fun
we are so worried
about what others think
that we forget to live
we forget
to take that leap of faith

#StartLiving

Acknowledgment

Thank you to singer-songwriter Tara Formosa for contributing "Summer Fling" to this collection and for inspiring me to write "Hot Girl Summer."

....

Thank you for reading! If you'd like to share your thoughts, please connect via my socials.

Instagram: heartstrings_hashtags
Tiktok: heartstringshash

www.ingramcontent.com/pod-product-compliance
Lightning Source LLC
La Vergne TN
LVHW052051160826
845678LV00015B/3177

* 9 7 8 1 7 3 8 4 5 8 9 7 4 *